MW00895851

The Essential John Reibetanz

The Essential
John Reibetanz

selected by Jeffery Donaldson

The Porcupine's Quill

Library and Archives Canada Cataloguing in Publication

Reibetanz, John, 1944 –
[Poems. Selections]
    The essential John Reibetanz / selected by Jeffery Donaldson.

(Essential poets series)
Poems.
ISBN 978-0-88984-406-3 (softcover)

    I. Donaldson, Jeffery, 1960 –, editor II. Title. III. Title: John
Reibetanz. IV. Series: Essential poets (Erin, Ont.)

PS8585.E448A6 2017   C811'.54   C2017-904716-7

1   2   3   •   19   18   17

Published by The Porcupine's Quill, 68 Main Street, PO Box 160,
Erin, Ontario NOB 1TO. http://porcupinesquill.ca

Represented in Canada by Canadian Manda.
Trade orders are available from University of Toronto Press.

We acknowledge the support of the Ontario Arts Council and the Canada
Council for the Arts for our publishing program. The financial support of
the Government of Canada is also gratefully acknowledged.

Table of Contents

Transformations (2006)

Afloat (2013)

Where We Live (2016)

Foreword

'Of man's first disobedience and the fruit of that forbidden tree ...'
(slight pause) 'whose mortal taste brought death into the world and
all our woe, with loss of Eden ...' (another pause) 'til one greater man
restore us and regain the blissful seat ...' (longest pause) 'Sing!
heavenly muse.' John Reibetanz sits casually on the desk at the front
of the classroom. The year is 1980: a course on the Romantics at
Victoria College. Reibetanz is on. He wants to be there. He is
making a point about poetic inspiration and how our understanding
of its origins has changed over time. The muses were once thought,
in Milton for instance, to be outside us, a mastery of voice that might
descend from metaphoric heavens if we listened aright.

Our teacher had simply lowered a bucket into a private well
called 'lines that have stayed with me' and come up with a splash
of Milton. I was dazzled. A literature at the tip of your tongue!
The performance itself was sufficient to impress my memory. But as
I think back to how *essential* John Reibetanz has been to my own
sense of poetic journey, I see another possibility. To a restless
twenty-year-old, Toronto in the 1980s seemed so ordinary, so plainly
there, so unequal to a youthful hungering for imagination's 'more'.
Here was a kind of solution. The creative impetus is both within us
and around us, at the same time, as poetry itself is. Reibetanz was my
proof in the pudding. Milton and others served Reibetanz as Milton's
muse had once served Milton, as a wellspring from without. And just
so, those otherworldly ardours become here and now effective in an
active imagination: the inheritance becomes an inhering. I had my
exemplar and I wasn't letting go.

Little did I know in that class of 1980 that Reibetanz was then
embarking on journeys of his own, journeys into family and poetry,
that would carry him through the inner and outer worlds of their
abiding concerns. I propose two keys to Reibetanz's imaginative
cosmology (the achievement is spacious enough to accommodate
alternatives ...) and not surprisingly they are intertwined. On the
one hand, you will find expressed throughout this volume the sense
of family and community as a willed construction, the bonds that
one *makes up one's mind* to build out of whatever resources are
provided (meagre or plentiful); it is the work, in every sense, of

7

affection. On the other hand, one sees that same sense of grapple applied to the age-old contest—occupying the mind of every poet, willy-nilly—between matter and mind, the heavy facts of the material world weighed against imagination's lift.

In Reibetanz's first book, *Ashbourn*, we find both motifs. In 'Lewis Bolt, Farmer' a wrestling with 'muckheaps' (Stevens's 'Man on the Dump'?) becomes a means of making oneself at home, starting with foundations, where a determination to 'crop that rock' aligns counterintuitively with a willingness to keep moving (the mystery of always turning to fresh tasks that we find, for instance, in 'The Wood-Pile' by Robert Frost, a 'near relation'). This is no surprise. With an itinerant childhood passed among relatives in Queens, Brooklyn, then New Jersey, then Manhattan and Brooklyn College, the poet himself was kept moving throughout his childhood, in difficult circumstances hinted at in 'Lincoln Logs' (*Near Relations*). You build a home out of the pieces that are given you. Reibetanz doesn't shy away from naming the pieces that he built with, however grim.

This idea in *Ashbourn* of subjects making themselves up, as it were, found its exemplary forebear in Richard Howard's collection of dramatic monologues, *Untitled Subjects*, which won the Pulitzer Prize for poetry in 1970. Howard's exploration of the genre, made famous by Robert Browning in the nineteenth century, focuses on questions of history and how individuals try to name a place for themselves in relation to it. The dramatic monologue is a poem of process, a kind of wrestling ring where a speaker—both revealing and withholding—gets actual psychological work done there and then as it speaks. Reibetanz swaps out Howard's and Browning's sense of an unintentional confession and adds the role of community in the work of self-creation. The villagers in Ashbourn speak both for themselves and for the abiding relations that bind them in the actual and imaginative communities they inhabit. That sense of a poem as a community of voices has remained with Reibetanz throughout his career and may explain how he could make himself so quickly at home in Canada when he arrived here in 1968. His early scholarly work shows him reading and assimilating the examples of a generation of Canadian poets, including E. J. Pratt, James Reaney, Jay Macpherson, and Dennis Lee. The reimagining of poetic narrative in this northern movement provided Reibetanz with a valuable alternative to the typographically and thematically narrow poetry then in vogue in the States.

Reibetanz's sense of the autobiographical weaves its way between two further landmarks in historically particular verse, Robert Lowell and Elizabeth Bishop. His belief that the sometimes harshly historical can be honest grist for the poetic mill points him in the direction of Lowell. At the same time, a deeper sense of discretion, a belief that personal experience — though it be fraught with peril — should not be confessed so much as exemplified, aligns him with Bishop. So in a poem like 'What Just Was' (*Near Relations*) — where the intertwined endings and beginnings of life float indiscreetly past the poet's attention — the point clearly is not to 'make a scene', but to make something *of* a scene. Distilled from Lowell too are those towering syntactical edifices, always upping the ante, the throw of a single momentum borne for stanzas: poetry as *bel canto*. Distilled from Bishop is the sense of the eidetic particular, the primacy of the image, the burden of innocent descriptive *capture* resting on every moment. At the root of all vision (its double meaning reminds us) is a thing well seen.

It is part of Reibetanz's dexterity in using autobiography that the hells and heavens of personal history in a poem like 'A Chest of Angels' (from *Midland Swimmer*) can morph seamlessly into a meditation on larger scopes, where we scout out the sacred within the secular, the otherworldly in the midst of the dystopian. The pun on the word 'chest' in the title gives us our formula, where a pop cooler in a Brooklyn garage and a heart filled with the need to make more of it provide the productive tension. The spiritual stakes are never far from these poems. The Greek term *kairos* has come to mean something like 'fullness of time', or the decisive moment in which the physical world opens to the metaphysical world, or where, in a poem like 'Points of Reference', the national opens onto the mythic. Much of Reibetanz's verse can be seen as a meditation on the state of mind and the exact verbal conditions that might render a poem ready and waiting for such transformation.

Wallace Stevens has provided many poets of the post-war generations with terms for the imagination's confrontation with reality. I think of Reibetanz's 'The Wood Bird' in relation to Stevens's

9

'Of Mere Being' for instance, where the bird (both imagined *and* real ...) that sings in 'the palm at the end of the mind' becomes now nature's 'subtle decoy' for human artifice. The 'idiot-savant' of the material world randomly tosses up masterpieces that require only our own 'imperfect vision' to see it thus. Sculpture comes to bear here, where a kind of fixed swirling in Reibetanz's poetry aligns it with the tensions of stone and water, the concrete and the fluid, the hardened and the dehiscent. The imagination partakes of, and enters into, nature's own dialectic, and finds itself there both chastened and fulfilled. Fixed forms fall into play with the verbal momentums that pass through them. Every sentence dilates and directs, wends its way by coursing among islands of concentrated wordplay.

The arc of Reibetanz's career to date reaches after a genuine self-transcendence, as exceptional achievements often do: the struggle to be different from oneself. Hegel used the term 'Aufhebung' to underline the three paradoxical conditions for success: to rise above, to leave behind, and to preserve. I follow Reibetanz's most recent work (in *Afloat* and *Where We Live*) with intense interest and observe how his exploration of the ancient Chinese masters, for instance, has informed his webbing. The tercets open out horizontally; punctuation marks are replaced by airier lacunae; shuttling phrase-parcels become discrete building blocks, at once reticulated and continuous, balancing acceleration and impedance. The poems, for all their heft and polish, seem to move towards ... movement itself. Looking for continued inspiration, Reibetanz reminds us that originality lies, wherever else, in an exploration of origins, water returning to its source. And as with most sources of inspiration — a verse form, a voice taken to heart, a world of stone and water — the fact that they are not easily possessed is part of what makes them inspiring. To rise above, to leave behind, and to preserve is the mission of any poet of Reibetanz's mettle, exacting enough to be essential. Sing, heavenly muse.

Lewis Bolt, Farmer

A rat caught in a trap by the foot
Will gnaw it off for freedom, but
There are men who'll no more part with
Their chains than with the air they breathe.
Watching them sickens me: they throw
Body and soul into making each furrow
Straight as a knifeblade, as if it mattered —
Would the harvest be less if the furrows wavered?
Look: Toby Green's been fussing with that stretch
Of fence all day — he's got to touch
And wind the wires just so, you'd think
He was tuning fiddle strings. No spunk —
His hands go fiddling his life away.
We were boys together, and Toby
Played all the games; my hours were ruled
And filled like ledger pages — my childhood
Knew discipline, and that has made
Me the man I am. Pride
You may call it, but I have built
This farm out of a muckheap: Bolt's
Bog they called it, and thought me mad,
Throwing money hard come-by into the mud.
First I tackled the hedgerows — towering
Walls like a fortress, and you couldn't bring
A plough near them with the bloody roots
Running thirty-five feet across. A few fights
Between them and a bulldozer upped the acreage.
Next came the barn, netted with age-
Old binder string wound around nails rusted
Brittle; incredible the space wasted
By that and the other rubbish I cleared.
Finally the hands: I paid more, and hired
The best in the district, but after a struggle —
The Eleventh Commandment was not to haggle
For wages, as if working on one farm bound
A man to it for life; they don't understand

That work is just something to be done and paid for
And loyalty needn't enter the picture.
My first harvest neared, and the road
Swarmed with neighbours' cars; you could read
The thoughts behind their looks: was I steel,
Or would I give like soft metal?
A bit of a crash makes them feel less
Desperate about their own failures
And proves that a man who breaks with the old
Ways will never thrive. I did.
I have done well enough to buy my parents
Their own house, and give him an allowance
To do little chores. People ask if he
Minds — a daft question, really:
He is proud of me, and when you have spent
Your life sweating in the fields you want
To escape. It's only in the fog of pub-talk
That people want the old days back.
You mustn't get caught in a rut: now I've
Proved my worth here, I might move
On. Yes, I dream of the north:
Think of drawing a plough through earth
Hard as granite, to make it take
The shape you choose! I'll crop that rock.

Wendy

We float on the tides of each other's breath,
Diving in and out of sleep. Rod's arm
Rocks gently with my swells, and underneath
The currents of his pulse, mine is calm.
Do seabirds leave a wing unfurled to claim
White peaks of sea-dreams? He and I tonight
Flew most high when we hugged our earth most tight,
And love's warm yeast raised us above dreams.
Yeast floats on every wind, but who can find
Its secret? Air is all holes; and yeast,
Too quick for sluggish soil to keep it, lights
On a grape's dusty skin and kindles wine.
And love makes wine from vulnerable dust:
The heart's wounds open and close on it.

Sunday Morning Raspberry Picking

The rusty Chevy pickup brakes, nestling.
Before the engine cuts, 'You better believe—'
Drawls in hillbilly from the radio
And hangs a severed edge on the silence.
Clouds of road-dust settle. They are raised
Again when the next wheels mutter along the grooves.

This is no Lovers' Lane: the cars and trucks
Queue up bumper-to-bumper, funeral-style,
Thick sheers of mist lining the rear windows
In privacy the sun will soon dissolve.
Though friends and neighbours, all sit contained
Like focused athletes hunkered on a track.

At seven sharp, the owner's son unbolts
And swivels the chainlink gate. A dozen engines
Kick in, and the procession lumbers over
Hummocky ground, prints ancient mud in potholes,
And congregates at the first long bramble row
Where another son waits with baskets and directions.

True hand-me-downs of battered lime-green cardboard,
The baskets keep the stains of last year's harvest
Like frescoes cast by floods. Only slowly
The deeper red of fresh pickings rises
Over the fringe: small, edible briar roses,
The raspberries hide their blush with screens of thorns.

It is a sacrifice. Farmers owl-eyed from haying
Could hug their beds like cut grass; wives don't need
A rouge of stings and scrapes; nobody ever
Needs raspberries. Yet, a hunger burrows
Beneath their needs, sharp-clawed, and it will not
Be stilled until it surfeits on their pains.

Light sharpens and begins to trim their shadows
As mists of chatter rise from little circles
Throughout the patch. Now, from the shadowed grooves
Of heavy faces, a holiday laughter flashes
Too quick to lighten them, and focuses
Clutches of sweet, perishable rubies.

Body Language

'Your bodies may at last turn all to spirit …
If ye be found obedient.' (Raphael to Adam, *Paradise Lost* V)

These stones my feet spank making tracks
along the beach,
or, when I monkey around catching my breath,

the ones I scoop and wing
skipping up against
the waves' endless downward rolling steps,

will still be shuffling around here after
flights of tides
have worn away my body's feathery downs

and ground its chalk caverns and peak
to a fine talc.
Yet you, Raphael, in your waterproof

plumage of light, come tempting
with a sweet nothing —
a shadow fruit, a lifesaver all hole.

Where would I be without this
slippery parapet's
bony foothold? Cast to perfection in

a paralytic promised land:
never to wade
ploughlike through shingle, never to quicken into

a run, the heart's breakers pounding
their ribbed seawall
in an old salt rapport of blood and waves;

never to ride the crest
when hunger, love, or sheer
buoyancy ups and floods through every pore,

spirit turned all to body,
the irrepressible
ape beating my sweaty chest. Wingless,

our sense of who we are rises
like steamclouds from
the body's rockbound shore, and if we float

too far from land, the wind un-
plaits the rigging of
our fleetest craft, and drowns us in thin air.

We share the sea's need to ride up
against an end,
a wall of stone that takes our heave and impact,

leaves legendary floodmarks
sparkling in wet script,
and holds our full-pitched runs in echo chambers.

No crafty serpent tempted man.
In the beginning,
God set the apple in our chest, its flesh

red to the core, and from our rib
God shaped a mate
of bone, to hug us through high seas of time.

A Chest of Angels

'I have always felt that desolation,
that hell itself, is most powerfully expressed
in an uninhabited natural landscape
at its bleakest' — Anthony Hecht

I.

To each his own hell. Mine was an uninhabited
landscape as far from nature as you can get
without actually leaving the planet, a man-made

moon waste on Sixth Avenue in Brooklyn,
fired in the sun's kiln through unending
afternoons when I was nine or ten.

I can never get the whole scene put together
in my head, thanks to whatever guardian
spirit flags down potentially dangerous

intruders on the verge of memory,
but parts of me hold parts of it: my ears
play out the hissing wires' repeated rise

and fall, dry waves breaking above pavement;
my nostrils chafe where fumes of gasoline
weep from soft tarred patches in the asphalt;

through a chainlink grid, my eyes take in
some lot's trapped beach, its black sand an amalgam
of gravel, soot, and broken glass; or they blink

in sequence with the traffic light's perpetual
solitaire at a carless intersection,
flicking over greens, ambers, reds;

my hands remember enough not to touch
the shut steel trap doors of delivery chutes
where air trembles over surfaces

as at their beginnings in a furnace.
What fills my mind to bursting is emptiness,
the spirit of inverted Genesis

transforming light and water's urge towards fullness
into a miracle of unearthly loss.

2.

Sentries, a pair of gasoline pumps napped.
Their rubber arms dangled groundwards and looped
back up, hanging slack from the brass lapel

their trigger-fingers hooked at shoulder height.
They were no angels, but kept the gate of hell
whenever I made visits to the angels.

Behind them, next to a roll-up garage door
always rolled up, with an invisible car
always risen above the stone lintel

on the hydraulic lift, a soft drink cooler
sat coffin-like against the stucco wall.
And always songs from a hidden radio

promised cool mountain rivers to the hot
flat city: somebody else must have listened,
but I never saw a soul in all my visits.

The angels' wings fluttered the moment I raised
the lid, a potent shimmer, as if the sun
itself shone from the chest, not its reflections

playing off the steel bars and icy waters.
The angels sat in rows between the bars,
their orders chevroned by the shapes and colours

of their glass capes: the bluish, scalloped whorl
of cherubim, the powers' straight sheer crystal,
the emerald flare of flaming seraphim—

all emissaries from the sky-washed shore
of heaven. To put a coin in the dispenser,
slide one of them along its plated channel

and lift it free through the chest's narrow gate—
to kiss the cold stars of its distillation—
was not important; it was only important

to see the angels swimming in the glitter
and dip my fingers in their flickering water
at the centre of that man-made desert,

knowing that they were man-made, and might shatter.

The Wood Bird

Crazed with patterning,
the world surrounds us with
more grains than fingers can trace,
more watery channels than imagined
plunges by the thinnest midge can slip through,
worlds within the world, each with its seas
filling with rivers that spill from jungles too ravelled
for the footwork of the most acrobatic mindwalker.

I nearly landed on it:
running along a beach swept clean
as a prepared canvas by the retreating tide,
eyes far ahead, ready for nothing underfoot
but the sand's moist, slightly springy flatness,
I sidestepped in mid-stride to avoid
something sensed as shadow presence, flicker
on the unfocused edge of vision.

Curiosity and a tender ankle
spurred by the near miss, I limped back. Beached
nose-in, like a newly landed canoe,
a hand-sized object had been washed ashore.
Thin neck, whorled sides devolving
to a ridged splay that could be tail feathers:
dead bird or driftwood? It appeared too wooden
to be a bird, too birdlike to be wood.

I picked it up: the nearly weightless
firmness I gripped gave surety to my hand
that what I held was not the softening wreckage
of feather and flesh, but hard-edged woodwork
hewn and shaped by the water's buffetings
into this subtle decoy. The shiver
that might have followed a more savage find
came on now, its strength surprising me.

Fingerless, blind, the waves had carved
and planed, distressed and sanded the wood
until its hairline frets and the tiered ridges
of its grain took on the nap of layered feathers,
a fine, impenetrable velvet where the heart
would lodge, taper then flaring to the coarser folds
of a tail's drapery: it was mindless drift's
winged masterpiece,

and its perfection shook me.
I could accept a world bent on destruction,
floodwaters gutting foundations, filling
word-shaping mouths with formlessness — a storm
for the flexed wing to rise above, darkness
starved for the light it wolfs down; but to find
tooled intricacy fashioned and then tossed out
indifferently as scrap, dumped on the sand

to be picked up or not
as chance might have it, left me at a loss,
landed with the driftwood bird
under inaccessible sky. The world
had turned unbalanced and vulnerable,
idiot-savant living from hand to mouth,
dependent on the imperfect vision of
a lame runner on an empty beach.

Points of Reference

They are brothers: this cruciform
subway sign at Yonge and King
(the lettered rectangle of head beaconing
from a trunk of tubular aluminum)

and the *inuksuk*, a subarctic man
made up of stones banked up
on the tundra's level drift, companionless
as an astronaut abandoned on the moon.

Blood brothers: their kinship stems
not from the common humanoid
shell they both shadow,
but from an impulse intimate as semen,

invasive as ink. The limblike strokes
of the *inuksuk*'s granite hieroglyph
and the stick-letters of graffiti
scratched in the pillar's metal bark

inscribe a will not to be defeated
by the unreadable line
of the dumb world's incomprehension,
either stretched out so taut it flattens

the landscape to one slit of horizon,
or stiffened into glaciated scarps
that crib the sky.
Where no song rises to astound

the asphalt's roaring cataract
or melt the permafrost, their mute
language digs in, defending points
of reference, marking beachheads on a hostile

void, reading matter for travellers
who take passage across blank waters
or descend by escalator
to ride the lines of shadow rivers.

June Light

This pink light so thick
　one might swim in it
　　anchors the morning's

uncargoed ship. It's
　right that later light
　　will thin as the day's

freight accumulates,
　letting the vessel
　　slip its moorings, gain

open water and
　taper from sight in
　　light, dwindling and pink.

Christmas Pageant

Instead of leaves
   the fresh snow cleaves
    to apple branches.

Sun will bring fall
   by noon, in small
    avalanches

of white applause
   where choruses
    of blossom swing.

I know the wet
   snow packs a threat:
    its weight may ring

the curtain down,
   too heavy a crown
    bow the king.

But robed with dawn
   the tree puts on
    an act of spring.

Kaleidoscope

The world had not yet set:
it shifted and rippled
like wind-dimpled water
or water-curtained wind.

Clothespegged to the wheelframe,
flapping against the spokes,
a playing card became
a motor for a bike.

Toppled over, the tall
rectangular cardboard
box from a just-installed
fridge or washer lumbered

along the ground — our tank,
powered by hands and knees
that rode each side's jackknifed
collapse to the pavement.

In stoopball, our batter
was a sandstone step's edge:
rubber balls pitched at it
would thwack across the surge

of cars and buses down
four lanes, invisible,
and then — like manna — find
hands cupped for miracles.

I lay in bed one night
and turned over my room
by staring at the white
ceiling until it seemed

a cleared-off, spotless floor;
and as I thought my foot
over the raised doorway,
I saw again the white

chalkline someone had drawn
that afternoon around
my friend, the other John,
who'd curled up on the ground

and looked like sleeping since
a bus caught him before
he'd time to catch my hit.
I wondered how the hard

asphalt had let him pass
through to another world,
where thought's turns rose and rose
like upward waterfalls.

Mel's Barn

In memory of F. Melville Caswell, 1913–1996

God must have lived there — heaven knows
it was too big to be a human house:
so high it brewed its own weather of mists
and captive rainbows up around the roofbeams,
where light hung polished from the fissures
in an arsenal of spare thunderbolts.

Outside, its timbered walls lorded
like sheer grey rock over the lesser hills
of neighbouring farms, even when the light
of aging winter afternoons softened
the roof peak's ice-blade, sheathing slopes
of burnished snow in watery deep blue.

In winter storms it was less ark
than harbour, a fixed anchorage when squalls
sank the horizon and raked fields shifted
their whitecapped tides. Cold sucked Mel's chimney smoke
up a thin siphon, but the barn
would hold its breath and stay under for weeks.

Mel was the barn's man: he belonged
to it. He oiled the great barred jaw's hinges,
and swept up scraps from heaped wagons that shivered
over the ramp's threshold, load after load
into the insatiable gloom.
He stacked its ribbed galleries with blond fuel,

and in return the barn killed Mel
by inches. As he aged, it gathered all
the years of dead weights he had lifted, heaved
its giant mass behind them and bore down
in fury on his joints. It breathed
fumes of ripe silage over him; quickened,

old threshing dust arose in clouds
and ate like locusts through the reddening
fields of his lungs. It fastened on his heart
failing wingbeats left among the rafters
by generations of trapped birds
whose flights south ended in its leafless wood.

Nothing the barn could do weakened
Mel's love for what it held and what it gave.
It held the wind's tide, dry as running grain,
bodying him and piping through the eaves
until their vents became his ears —
his thoughts drawn into sound, his mind grown choir.

The barn gave what his eyes took in
whenever he climbed its back and found again
a tiered world waiting there, brimming around him
as bright as if the sun had poured the hills
minutes before and they, all shimmer,
hung fire, too filled with being to be still.

Acolyte in bibbed overalls,
what could he do, the night a spear of light
pierced the barn's head and brought it down in flames,
but stare at nothing over the charred wood —
too loyal to defect to blind
chance, and too old to raise another god.

Lincoln Logs

Once upon a time. A six-year-old boy
  almost might be raising himself
from the waters of sleep, onto a beach
  made glass as a wave's sheet pulls taut.
His left arm props his torso, his legs (still
  sleeping?) trail behind like a seal's
footless, tapered shank. Almost: but the gloss
  this beach holds is the solid flow
of a waxed floor, and the boy's eyes — open,
  their own glitter fully wakened —
focus on his right hand about to crown
  an afternoon's labour. He holds
a wooden cube and sets the inverted
  carved V of its base in triumph
on a green cardboard roof: the log cabin
  has its chimney. He has built well,
linking the dovetailed, pencil-thick pieces
  of squared cedar, blocking out
the door and windows, even contriving
  an alcove where his frontiersmen
will hang their coonskin caps and long rifles.

There is so much he doesn't know. If his
  ignorance were a log, its weight
would crush him. He has no idea his mother,
  who reads *The Deerslayer* to him
while he builds, lives mostly in a country
  called madness, and her body will
spend the next two years in an asylum.
  He doesn't know that the gleaming
linoleum floor will fail to hold him,
  giving way to spare-room sofas,
basement daybeds, fold-ups, as he's shunted
  from hand to ever-more-remote
hand in the family's bucket brigade.

He won't realize for decades
that the last few distant uncles and aunts
    are paid strangers, and even the
logs' honest 'Lincoln' is a hollow pun.

Yet, he doesn't need your pity or mine.
    He sees the mirroring water
doubling the cabin's height is Glimmerglass,
    the lake where Deerslayer held off
marauding Hurons in his log refuge.
    He senses it's in the reflected
cabin that Cooper's 'dark chest' holds the secret
    of who we are. He is the boy
who will open the cardboard cylinder
    of Lincoln Logs in every room
he lands in, building his cabin again
    and again. The boy who floats
in his white jersey like smoke pluming from
    the chimney, or like the genie
of a tale he's read on his own, set free
    from a bottle that can't hold him.
Who will learn — or does he need to learn? —
    the answer to a nightmare is
to build a cabin on a sheet of water,
    sinking the pencil-thick supports
into the fathomless centre of a dream.

She Goes Like

It's character assassination time
next to Captain Video, at Mr Game's
arcade. Cool neon surf breaks over them,

green and purple rippling the metal O's
on lip or lobe. They breathe out a clear gas
of words to warm themselves. Ashley's exposed

navel shivers when they start in on Mr.
Spinelli's homeroom or his history classes.
Her mind fast-forwards *You should've seen the bastard*

this morning, stops, rewinds her eyes catching
his in World Civ sliding down her cleavage.
No, too gross: eject. Instead: 'His clothes,

they're like so Yesterday.' Safe choice, that place
half underground, walls papered with dead names,
the living room of all the guys' parents.

There, Ashley wears the name Anton and Eva
fit her into when she was only a dream,
in the Budapest whose air their dreams still breathe.

'Elektra.' Imagine. Years of getting called
'Lightbulb' or 'Hydro' in elementary school
sent her off to Central Tech as Ashley.

She broke it to them slowly. They have a thing
about new things — whatever some Hungarian
fossil didn't invent or eat. Anton's

instrument hatelist targets electric shavers,
digital watches, Japanese violins.
'And Eva goes like *Peanuts butter isn't*

a launch. Cheese isn't cheese unless it reeks.
Forget about sushi.' She cringes when they talk,
their tongues caught up on consonants sticky

with foreign memories. Yet tonight, past one,
Ashley won't fall asleep till they come home
(the tables stacked, the door's sign switched to CLOSED)

and whisper the old world into her ear,
their breath threading with hers in endearments
like nothing spoken by her yesterday.

The Hammer

The mother whose hand trembled with his soft pounding
    inside her abdomen, marvelling that a complete
    new being could be contained within her,
whose hand guided to his mouth the first small spoon of food
    that did not come from her own body,
whose hand enveloped his hand as her body had once
    enveloped his, on morning walks to
    the school building where she
    would deliver him again,

would not as I have done this morning walk staring past
    the outstretched upraised dirty hand that juts
    like a downspout from this building,
would not have marvelled even so at his ingenuity
    in fitting himself and all his worldly goods
    into a diagonal niche between two storefronts,
but would look down at her own hand, beyond marvelling
    that such a miraculous contrivance could clench
    itself into a thing, and pound and pound.

What Just Was

The road to school was the closest I came to death:
darkness welled and clotted, a tar pool
you could just by some miracle breathe through.

Michaela had come closer. Her father, hoping
to sleep his way out of debt, turned on the gas
and scuttled himself, his wife, their mortgaged house.

Now she lived with her aunt on my side of town.
We met mornings to walk to school, running
where the road ran through the cemetery.

It wasn't just the shuddering of branches
around and above: drawn down between
high banks, the road caved in to rooted gloom,

and behind the iron fence, a downward pull
levelled the raised loaves of fresh plots
and sucked older headstones deep into turf—

something under the groomed nap seething
with a will to extinguish. On the walk home, high sun
broke the spell enough for us to risk

slipping in past a bowed iron fencebar
to take a shortcut over gravelled footpaths
to another gap at the far end. We crossed

a stream you couldn't see from the road, feet
drumming the floorboards of the wooden bridge
to send a heartbeat through the mute village

of stonebound, narrow lanes.
                              Feeling bolder
one spring afternoon (the leaves still buds
letting light flood through), we paused on the bridge

and looked down from the highest point of the arch.
The stream ran swollen, glossy brown except
where rocks turned up tufted white patches

and, right below us, where a hidden whirlpool
of strong current spun under the bridge
and flung out water-diamonds from a pinwheel

just beyond sight. We hunched beneath the rails
and leaned over. Schooling up, circling
one of the creosoted pillars,

what looked like fat minnows bobbed and swayed,
riding the current. We looked again: not minnows.
Both too shy to say what we both saw —

the school of condoms: some flat, some distended
with water, all dancing — we watched in silence,
red-faced with shame, and with an awkward sense

of something stirring within us like what stirred
below: a pulse, rising from our own dark parts,
that would grow strong enough to carry us

clear out of childhood. Unforgettable
dance, unthinkable to talk about
as her lost parents, an obscenity

we bowed to every afternoon that spring
in the same hushed, innocent homage.
                                    Nothing
earthshaking came of it — soon we went on

to different schools, lost touch — nothing except
the going on itself, a flowing through earth's
nothing on something human that just was.

Torch Singer

In the forest, long
after its tables
of sunlight have been
cleared, after the small
cricket ensembles
have packed up and left
and rows of cushioned
toadstools sit empty,
she comes in, the old
woman who washes
the floor and sings what
you know are the blues
because her low notes
coat the pine needles
with indigo and
the lyrics matter
less than the cloudy
refrains of sorrow
that sweep across but
never stifle this
torch song of love so
long unrequited
she has become the
torch she holds, a stone-
faced, dry-eyed, bald but
white-hot soprano.

What We Owe the Stars

1. We must start lower, with what we owe the boulder:
debt-burden, heaped silt sloughed from the floods of many
generations. We tote it up by climbing back

   into our mothers' bodies, as they into theirs
hitching a ride on the chain drawn back in through them
to the stone age where sedimented sand began

   to impart its lessons in patience. In return,
since we are still too skittish to repay in kind,
we will feel the warmth it can't when the sun bathes it.

2. Nor will our debt to water ever be discharged
no matter how much we give back to the oceans
of what we take from the rain, for we embezzle

   at all its ports of call. Eyes loot the waterfall's
downcast face, and siphoning mouths mime in reverse
fountain's overpayment to basin. Only, when

   water teeters mutely at a cup's lip, our lips
can part and, on the brim of our utmost plunder,
give its insatiable soul a voice in our 'aah'.

3. We owe most to the stars who, possessing neither
stone's unwavering bastions nor water's slippery
cape of invisibility, have soldiered deep

   into death's cold country, diminutive cadets
each holding only a small candle for defence.
We owe it to them to love each other and launch

   our blood-warmed breath to secure their farthest outposts:
then the stars will stop shivering with loneliness
and the night will close its eyes on sleep like a stone.

Speech Therapy

His love speaks the language of love
more lithely than the sage linguists.
Her lips and teeth negotiate
its iterative straits and twists
as fleet as neon pulsing through
the uncials and cursives of
the night's calligraphy.
                              Her love
speaks volumes with his hands, grasping
the branching, transformational
syntax and deep structure of
a dialect of rounded vowels.

Their love's a love of discourse held
in conversations where, amid
a theory of performance and
a generative grammar all
fricative and labial,
the tongue's licked into shape.

The Love of Water

All nature, from the crag windbreakered in granite
that melts into the nuzzling of the clouds' wet snouts,

to the motes of grit that rise up every morning
and dance in a fountain over the windowsill,

all nature wants to be water. Curled tongues of fire
and sharp tongues of wind stutter and lisp through forests,

longing for the fluency of streams. Clays trapped in
marble fifty million years ago still practice

ripple and purl in rehearsal for the aeon
that will free their liquid hearts, Virginia creeper

clambers on splay-fingered hands up walls and tree trunks
to throw itself down in cascading sprays, even

heaven seeks out lakes where its unfrozen double
pulses. Still more besotted, water dotes on the rest

of nature. Rain, the sky's gift of spirit, so pure
a distillate of blue it abstains from colour,

falls all over the earth, and snowflakes leave unique
designs they've spun their lives into, coming undone

to kiss the same ground the river's whitest water,
charging seaward, turns inside out to wave back at.

Starving for love, the pilgrim waterdrop shivers
under its hood of light, dwindles to mist, and slips

into crevasses between crumbs of soil, to rise
as breath through root-hairs and be at one with the trees.

Or with you, for water also loves the nature
that is human. Kissing lips, then tongue, it races

down throat-rapids, threads through bone into your very
marrow and, in a blush of passion, spills over

and floods the heart's chambers scarlet. Your smitten heart
loves back, a lifetime of embraces fluttering

like eyelids when they caress the film of water
pressing against your lenses. You look through them at

a dead tree leaning across a stream. The bleached trunk
so yearns to become water, it has given up

branches and bark in working its way from cedar
to drift. Now pain puts on a coat of warm water

and runs down your cheek. Like the ocean that loved all
nature into first life, it kisses you with salt.

Bluegrass

starts with   mouth-to-mouth inspiration   from the beige-lipped
perfect   O   of a Martin D-28 guitar
where soul on rebound from plucked brass   swims up through sound waves

and waits humming behind a copse of hair   at the mouth
of an ear-cave   for the high lonesome sound   another
soul breaks into   when it breaks as breath   out of its white

ribbed chest-cave   slips on a jumpsuit of song   from the red
walls of the singer's mouth   rides the trilled riptide outwards
and partners its soulmate   to sashay down the vaulted

canal   career off tautened eardrum   toggle hammer
on anvil   and tickle the coiled-up cochlea   but
the true beginnings of bluegrass   echoed through ancient

rock caves whose high roofs   hummed duets with stone-age singers
enchanted by warm overtones   the icy limestone
draped around their solitary voices   longing to

prolong the partnership   between what lasts   and what runs
out of breath   seeking to carry harmony with them
as a body   out of the cave   finally lighting

on wood   carved into a heart shape   too full of singing
to taper to a point   curved like a woman gravid
with new music   soundboard braced by rosewood ribs   slim neck

drawing out voice cords   like drops of water drawn into
needles   wept from cave roofs   brimming with human sorrow
yet plucking joy   from hearing unhuman wood echo

their song in its own bright voice   even on starless nights
as if they had come   at the farthest reach of a cave's
dark passage   into a place of green skies   and blue grass

A Chinese River in Brooklyn

For Amy K. Epstein, its source

Like all New Yorkers   although at a remove
from lower Manhattan   she would shiver whenever
a banking plane's engines mimicked that targeted plunge

or sun-glare on the river mirrored the mirrored flames
or a burst of black smoke from some hidden chimney smudged
across white facades   so she will pardon my first sight

for having read holocaust behind the orange glow
and drifting haze of this landscape painting   which reflects
in its hush of white silk no disaster   but our shared

love for a thousand-year-old scroll by Dong Yuan   his
river valley and banked mountains   a beckoning depth
behind her watery strokes   his monochrome quickened

by her bright palette into this sunrise   where we perch
on the right foreground's rocky promontory   giddy
at the miles of air dangling from its two trees   bleary

with morning mist   down to the river below and out
to the muscled backs of distance-dwarfed mountain ranges
our giddiness witness to one of the miracles

of art   as an eleven inch square of silk draws us
out of narrow hemmed lives   into a thousand-year-wide
vista   lit by a still older sun's life-giving fire

The Vineyard

How long will it take, when my body is stored in the cask
of the earth, for hands to offer up the bone and muscle
of grasp and fist, and become the undulating, light-filled

fine-veined hands of vine leaves? How long for the backbone's steel shaft
to soften into a questioning whisper, coiling and
resting on whatever support the earth comes up with? How

many tides for thought to purge itself of edge and corner
and be poured into the sea-polished roundness of the grape's
sweet flesh? And how long before blood, shuttling through its tunnels,

becomes this unbound flowering, this blushing face that needs
no mirror because it is one, giving the world the world
dyed into rose heart and rising as the scent of morning.

Wash

'If you hide your boat in a canyon, and then hide the mountain
in a marsh, you may think the boat is safe and secure.
But something powerful might come in the dead of night,
heave it all onto huge shoulders and carry it away.'
                                        —Chuang Tzu (365–290 B.C.E.)

Let your boat wash away downstream   on the numbed current
of the drowned river   like a floating   spirit-laden
paper lantern   at the Feast of the Hungry Ghosts   on

to the next world   let the shoulders of its gunwales heft
on planks laid across them   like a bearer's yoke   the full
cargo of your losses   from small offerings you could

touch   a worn toothbrush   an outgrown shoe with one buckle
missing   to the ever unreachable hostages
of the deep   ghost of your face in window glass   among

plum leaves long fallen on steps of children's forgotten
games   white ghosts of child-breath over frost on a plum branch
and let your boat not capsize   under the greater heft

of streets you will never walk again   in old Wushan
Fengdu   Shibaozhai   under the stones of lost Fengjie's
West Tower   where Du Fu's ghostly finger still traces

the arc of a setting moon   round white stone   it lowers
itself onto the boat   ripples a silk scarf waving
farewell   but from the vast unmaking of this wash   may

                        * * *

making arise   as the heavenly dragon leaps up each
spring   from the river's jade dungeons   to race through veins of
peach and plum   and blossom as cloud-puffs   whose breath scatters

dead leaves   whose lightning-claws rake down rain   to wash away
winter   and slake the bare earth's thirst   or may creation
take the untouchable shape   of *hsien*   a flowering

of pure   spirit   brush-charactered as moonlight broken
free   from its black-wreathed tomb of white stone   a wash of light
through open courtyard gates   or let a fresh world's rivers

and mountains rise   unbrushmarked   from the light and dark wash
of ink   as in the earliest landscape paintings   gift
of artists   whose unsigned lives were boats that sailed away

into the currents of their art   leaving no more trace
than their hands left   on the monochrome's dappled waters
a making never hostage to the river   never

seeking to cage the dragon   grasp the moonlight   or drink
from streams flowing down a silk scroll   where the no-colour
black   rainbows your washed eye   with all the floating colours

Curious George Takes Flight, 12 June 1940

That red balloon on a string   is really his heart   how
else will it carry him so far   how else will it lift
Margret and Hans with him   this morning they lower him

into a basket   like the infant Moses   swaddled
in overcoats   to float beside their bike wheels   sidling
through rushes of cars   taxis   horse-drawn wagons   people-

stocked pickups   along cobbled *allées*   where days from now
Nazi tanks will rattle   while Hans and Margret pedal
George can only sit   holding his balloon   in a tree

on the cover drawing   of their still-unpublished book
infant   to be born abroad   image of his parents
those buoyant colours   from mother's Bauhaus lore   handed

down   and from father's Hamburg zoo sketchings   those trapeze
leaps   tonight they'll sleep on a barn floor   wake under stars
not needed   to find their way through lost Europe   for George

will lead them from his cover page   unborn child seeing
times unborn   how else could he have guided Hans's brush
to make his bony perch   prefigure in leaflessness

tree skeletons   of a firebombed Hamburg zoo   how else
would the Reys' drawings have imaged   in his sea voyage
to the 'big city'   theirs   four months from now   holding hands

at the ship's rail   as their gaze climbs   with primate sureness
the extended arm of Liberty   so George midway
through the manuscript   stands at a prow   his arms aping

the freedom   of a seagull's extended wings   this child
the parent   when Margret holds a monkey pose   or Hans
mimics treetop chatter while he draws it   George guides them

from flaming cities   through forests of pure animal
instinct   remote from possession   invulnerable
to occupation   leads them into his harmony

so deeply they draw the notes   in their children's songbook
as hearts strung on the bridge of Avignon   gives their hearts
the courage to redraft   a yellow star of reproach

into wearable sun   the yellow hat of rescue
teaches them   though they lack the thumb on his monkey foot
how to fly by gripping that string   tightly as he does.

Repurposing

The phoebe's eye   a star-kindled coal   lights on the base
of a rusted hurricane lantern and sees that un-
chimneyed hearth housing the nest she will weave like smoke from

moss and weed stems   while the carolina wren's crevice-
sweeping gaze recasts the crook of a tin pot canti-
levered from an icicle-draped window frame   into

her nestlings' cradle   and the ruby-throated humming-
bird   undaunted as white noise blizzards from power lines
over her wing-throbs   transmutes the frozen sea-green spume

of a glass insulator   with her tiny lens's
laser   into a soft hollow where small-bodied heat
can warm two snowdrop eggs to life   who says metaphor

is solely a lettered human art   if metaphor
means seeing within something that is   something that is
not yet   birds thread it through air with every flight   pleating

grass into high-pitched roundels   turning horsehairs into
the enjambed lines of their collections   the cliff swallow
a model of Virgilian patience   transposing

mouthful by mouthful   clay to build its monuments   swifts
like mystical poets   spinning steep nests from their own
insides   these compositions infused with touchable

substance such as earthbound singers can only aspire
to shape from the airy wisps of words   what wonder then
that others of our species   gatherers like the birds

can like them repurpose the world's denser offerings
and warm the smallest spaces with the eye's power to
transform   as Daniel in his one-room sixth-floor walkup

refires old bricks by filling each round hollow with wax
and wick   or peels labels to release gleam from empty
soup tins that send blue brimmings of lobelia over-

flowing onto an end table whose top once windowed
a lean-to and whose bicycle-wheel legs splay after-
noon sun into webbed glitter-nests on his wall   while Jen

two flights down   sets lamplight streaming through the wooden slats
of an inverted wastebasket onto the bookcase
she has framed from a stepladder   her books extending

the ladder's reach beyond her low-ceilinged room   the shelves
stretching its walls around clearings of space and mind   each
castoff reclaimed by these inner-city foragers

a chimney swift's egg that contains   written in darkness
beneath a shell of snow   the flickering early stars
its inmate   breaking through   will gather under spread wings

Navigating Springwater Township

I traverse Minesing Swamp while clad in
carpet slippers, fathom Orr Lake without
toe-testing, track the long hill to Anten
Mills from Flos in well under a minute.

With my index finger I dam rivers,
block sideroads, raze local airports, a God-
zilla on the rampage who can cover
green conservation areas in red

with a swish of marker, even collapse
the whole township by folding up the map:
pathetic fall, hollow apocalypse —
my hold only a paper tiger's grip.

Maps endow us with the ghost of power,
putting phantom landscapes within our reach
where no winds gather, no tree towers or
spreads shade, and rivers never overleap

their fine blue lines. This township of the mind
defaces place, burying Snow Valley's
white crystals under black letters, drying
Marl Lake to parchment. Allenwood's been de-

foliated, and Rainbow Valley Road
flattened, losing both arc and dip. I need
to touch the scabrous bark of a white oak
whose roots are in the earth, not in D3

or H6, finger silk hairs from a burst
milkweed pod on the monarch-kindling shore
of Nottawasaga's warm bay. I thirst
for a long draught of unmapped Springwater.

Transmigrations

'Imperious Caesar, dead and turned to clay,
Might stop a hole to keep the wind away.'
— *Hamlet*, 5.1

Or might be mouthed by a house martin   to be spit out
as a teardrop-shaped daub for the wall of its mud hut

just as a drop of Caesar's blood might be sucked into
the stabbing hypodermic shaft of a mosquito

to be in turn pecked and swallowed by a chickadee
and become   from plunging through its alimentary

ductwork   part of the shell housing an embryonic
black-capped chick   which will use its pointed egg-tooth to pick

a hole in the wall   recycling the shell's calcium
into a wingbone riding winds to its winter home

but you   Hamlet   homeless wanderer in the boneyard
pick up a hollow gourd   wind-harrowed cave   abandoned

nest of your childhood   clay too brittle to be reworked
and wish the jester could be repurposed   unburdened

of memory   that he might house only next spring's fresh
songs   echo-free   no sparrows fallen on the threshold

The Gate

Nature's immortals do not share your fixation
with limits. Air comes and goes slick as a whistle
through midnight drapes as through the sheers of noon,
slipping down into your lungs for a warm kiss

or surfing the cool wind-waves above walls.
Water rolls over shorelines, melting into sand
and rock alike. Fire's hundred-fingered hands
thread the carved spume of spindles, yet can bull-

doze buildings into its roaring mouth. Even
earthbound trees reach into unfenced clearings
of sky, mortal leaves chatting, oblivious,
ablush as autumn leads to white closure —

and what doomed sparrow does not trust its wings
will always lift it over the tallest hedge?
Only your eyes survey the acreage
of infinity and find a shut gate waiting.

Chainlinked with death, you garden the enclosed
expanse, tend air and name it with your breath,
make rain your sorrow's whispers to an earth
that cannot give voice to its own deep thirst,

and train the flames of your rage to speak as roses.
Minding leaf cadences that escape a tree's
cupped lobes, you call them song. Reading the thrust
of rising beak and wing in swooping leaves,

you call up coming spring through autumn's cage
where, from a fallen tree, you carve a gate,
place a hand on it, turn it like a page,
and enter a garden waiting for you beyond it.

The House of Myth: In Memory of Northrop Frye

'Mythical animals ... may be as essential for society as mythology itself ...
as characteristic for human beings as nest-building is for birds. The
stories seem to be different stories, but the underlying structure is always
the same, in any part of the world, at any time.' —Lewis Thomas

One of its distinguishing properties is to be
without property   no visible means of support
comings and goings unencumbered as they have been

through all times and places   from mouthblown dioramas
of Paleolithic hollows to the wind-unfurled
pennants configured on inaccessible mountains

spied by satellite   yet some highly documented
urban encounters in modern central Canada
mention a portal surmounted by flared oriel

flanked by frameless windows   the house roofed in thatch described
as gold weathered to grey   accounts vary on whether
it stands or rocks gently on its footings   what is known

of the interior   scholars have pieced together
from shards of paper that seem to have drifted down from
regions far above the house's higher stories   all

confirm however a vestibule that leaves no room
for small talk   giving way abruptly in a cascade
of stone steps to the core of the building   likened by

as many sources to a vast furnace room as to
a hall of ice or a salt mine   these discrepancies
no doubt symptoms of the same disorientation

that has identified such spaces the world over
with legends of a permeable wall   how the hand
of one explorer resting against roughcast passed through

and when pulled back out was a furred paw   how another's
foot emerged ungulate and cloven   as if the wall
possessed the power to erode evolved distinctions

between animal and human   in the manner that
the subterranean flood cited in the fullest
of crypt narratives causes those who breast its current

to turn amphibian   web-limbed and furnished with gills
for breathing the air at the heart of water   before
surfacing once more in human form at the ground floor

landing of the winding stair that is such houses' most
contentious feature   windpipe-like spiral belying
the straight lines of written site studies and extending

within so far beyond the height gauged by external
purview as to end in the clouds   confusion reigns in
all the known records of these storied upper levels

yet however implausibly all evidence points
to a garden at the top of the stairs   where either
women named for flowers or flowers named for women

dance in unbroken rings around a dreamer rooted
in that place   his hair rippling leaves   his breath keeping time
with their quick steps   following them through closed eyes   bemused

Fresco Magic

1. Pompeii

Look how they made walls vanish   not by running through them
Harry-Potter-style   but by painting them with what lay
beyond   hillsides of nimble-limbed olive trees dandling

clustered fruit from silver fingers   wind-furrowed wheatfields
squirrels lacing the nearby oak groves   and if you threw
wide the batten-framed shutters your eyes would be treated

not trumped   with flourishes setting inner and outer
in harmony   grace notes of lacquered vines in duet
with sun-gilded grapes   shadows bridging from garden dials

to gnomons atop enameled globes   not a still life
among them   all in motion   whether counterpointing
the sun's steady pace or quickened by the caperings

of torchlight   the builders not weighed down with all you know
about the heavy rain of pumice that melted roofs
muffled transoms and blinded windows   for they looked on

stone walls as wells of shifting light   their view not monu-
mental but moment-centred   waving wands of trowel
and brush to summon up a flute breathlessly upraised

for your fingering   or jug-eared Silenus reeling
from a column   or Aurora herself in mid-step
winking at you to join in the dance   now you see it

2. Villa Cicogna Mozzoni

His brother the Count and heir can't stand the place   too far
from wi-fi   women   and song   so Jacopo tends it
tending mostly meaning standing after the rains   perched

high on a rung   patching cracked stucco or shoring up
tipsy roof-tiles   to keep the damp from feasting on aged
plaster and making a velouté of the frescoes

composed in the 1560s by two craftsmen from
Cremona   whose art was brush rather than awl   and who
brought back through pigment-magic the century-old glow

of the Duke of Milan's visit   but Jacopo's most
cherished frescoes aren't *Young Agostino Mozzoni
Saves Duke Galeazzo from the Ferocious Bear*   or

the untitled bedroom panels whose red paint takes on
the nap and fall of velvet   or the hallway's presti-
digitation   where the marble balustrade your hand

reaches for dissolves into a flat mirror-image
of its solid counterpart   but rather those vistas
that open view on view like Russian dolls   the stone-browed

portal framing a hall whose floor tiles gleam with sunlight
from some unglimpsed window   and whose foreshortened walls frame
another hall   where three thin-thinner-thinnest rays lay

gold stripes across a narrowing blue runner that ends
before the smallest hall targets your eye on a nub
of window at its heart   or the scene most at *his* heart

perhaps because most exposed   outdoors where the arcade's
painted sky peeks through a painted trellis supporting
espaliered branches   bunches of grapes   and climbing hands

and feet of two putti grinning down from opposite
sides of the ceiling   each boy either upright or up-
side-down   grapes dangling or levitating   depending

on whose chubby-fingered grip you focus   Jacopo's
weathered hands touching all the magic   his feet knowing
the ache of keeping such laddered airiness aloft

About John Reibetanz

John Harold Reibetanz was born on July 28, 1944, in Queens, New York, the only child of Harold Reibetanz and Veronica Hanley. His mother worked as a teacher; while her struggles with depressive episodes occasionally required that the young Reibetanz be billeted with relatives, it was his father's career as a consulting engineer that kept the family on the move, apartment shifting from Brooklyn to Lodi, New Jersey, then to Brooklyn again and Manhattan, until Reibetanz attended Princeton University and graduated with his doctorate in 1968. It was at Princeton that Reibetanz had met his wife, Julia (Maniates), subsequently also a professor of English, specializing in 19th- and 20th-century literature at the University of Toronto. Having seen Julia in a reading room at Princeton, Reibetanz asked her out on a last-minute date. They stayed up talking until the small hours and a week later Reibetanz proposed. Their marriage on July 15, 1967, so close to Canada's centennial anniversary, seems to have predicted their 'coming home' to Toronto when Reibetanz joined the English department at Victoria College in 1968. 'I was not dodging the draft,' Reibetanz has said, 'but nevertheless renounced my American citizenship the first week we were here, as both an embrace of "here" and a protest against "there".'

Reibetanz's doctoral work centred on English Renaissance drama. His subsequent book on King Lear (*The Lear World: A Study of King Lear in Its Dramatic Context*) was published by University of Toronto Press in 1977 and nominated by the press for that year's Christian Gauss Award in criticism. His increasing interest in modern poetry and poetics was of a piece with his developing creative work. Since the early 1980s, he has studied contemporary poets and their use of traditional forms, with essays on such poets as Philip Larkin and Richard Wilbur.

The Reibetanz household grew apace through the 1980s with the birth of a daughter, Stephanie Sophia, then two sons, Timothy and David. The parents' devotion to family and community is amply evident in Reibetanz's work, where encounters with each child's uniqueness lent itself to a growth experience that is a part of the poetry's own evolution. The Reibetanzes' investment in community and its relation to the natural world was influenced, naturally, by their growing up in cities, but left them determined to expand their children's horizon of natural experience. The small farm they purchased near Creemore, Ontario, in 1980 (their summer home for fifteen years) takes a central place in the interpenetrating worlds of stone and water that anchor the poetry.

Reibetanz was the first recipient, in 1990, of the Victoria University Teaching Award. His courses in poetry and poetics, and increasingly in creative writing, underline his faith in learning as a creative activity, which, like a poem — as Horace prescribed — can instruct *and* delight. The classroom becomes a poetic space where thought may deepen and the poems one writes, far from seeming explicitly didactic, evince in turn a process of expanding consciousness by showing, not telling. The teaching award has complemented strong writing accolades. *Mining for Sun* was shortlisted for the ReLit Award in Poetry in 2001 and the poet was granted first prize in the international Petra Kenney Poetry Competition in 2002. Numerous individual poems have been singled out for distinction by the CBC, the Poetry Foundation's Archive, the National Magazine Awards, *Arc Poetry Magazine*, *The Fiddlehead* and *The Malahat Review*. John Reibetanz lives in Toronto.

Selected Bibliography

POETRY

Ashbourn, Signal Editions, 1986
Morning Watch, Signal Editions, 1995
Midland Swimmer, Brick Books, 1996
Near Finisterre, St Thomas Poetry Series, 1996
Mining for Sun, Brick Books, 2000
Near Relations, McClelland & Stewart, 2005
Transformations, Goose Lane Editions, 2006
Afloat, Brick Books, 2013
A Book of Riddlu, Aeolus House, 2015
Where We Live, McGill-Queen's University Press, 2016

CRITICISM

The Lear World: A Study of King Lear in Its Dramatic Context.
    University of Toronto Press; W. Heinemann, 1977.
'Theatrical Emblems in King Lear.' *Some Facets of* King Lear: *Essays
    in Prismatic Criticism*, ed. Rosalie L. Colie and F. T. Flahiff.
    University of Toronto Press, 1974: 39–57.
'"The Whitsun Weddings": Larkin's Reinterpretation of Time and
    Form in Keats.' *Contemporary Literature* 17, no. 4
    (Autumn 1976): 529–40.
'What Love Sees: Poetry and Vision in Richard Wilbur.' *Modern
    Poetry Studies* 11 (1982): 60–85.
'Philip Larkin: The Particular Vision of "The Whitsun Weddings".'
    Modern Language Quarterly 43, no. 2 (June 1982): 156–73.
'Lyric Poetry as Self-Possession: Philip Larkin.' *University of Toronto
    Quarterly* 54, no. 3 (Spring 1985): 265–83.
'Motherland: American Notes.' *Prairie Fire* 16, no. 3 (Autumn
    1995): 86–91.
'Molly Holden.' *Poets of Great Britain and Ireland Since 1960*.
    Dictionary of Literary Biography, Vol. 40, ed. Vincent B. Sherry, Jr.
    Gale Research Company, 1985: 238–44.
'Pier Giorgio di Cicco.' *Contemporary Poets*, 5th edition, ed. Tracy
    Chevalier. St. James Press, 1991: 223–24.

'Don Coles.' *Contemporary Poets*, 6th edition, ed. Thomas Riggs. St. James Press, 1996: 173–74.

INTERVIEWS

Interview: conducted by Ward McBurney, *Acta Victoriana* 113, no. 2 (April 1989): 12–17.
'John Reibetanz Past and Present: Two Interviews by John Clement Ball.' *Pan Del Muerto* 2 (Spring 1992): 3–9.
'The Magic of Ekphrasis: John Stintzi in Conversation with John Reibetanz.' *The Malahat Review* website: www.malahatreview.ca/interviews/reibetanz_interview.html